DISCOVER THE **MOST AMAZING TANKS** ON EARTH!

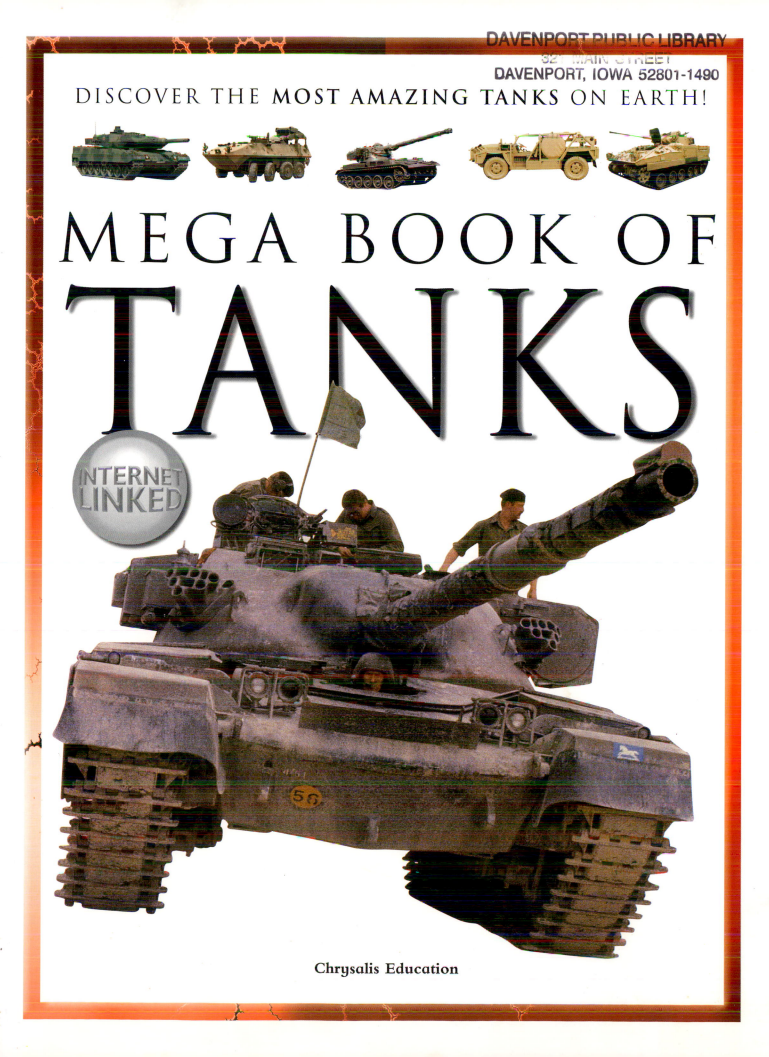

MEGA BOOK OF
TANKS

INTERNET LINKED

Chrysalis Education

INTERNET LINKS

http://wwii-allied-afvs.virtualave.net
This site provides specifications and detailed illustrations of tanks used by all the major Allied forces during World War II.

http://www.army-technology.com
Click on "Industry Projects" for international coverage of AFVs, artillery systems, attack and support helicopters, MBTs, missile systems, and much more.

http://www.battletanks.com
A collection of information and pictures of the major tanks from World War II to the present day.

http://www.fas.org/man
The website from the Federation of American Scientists provides detailed information on all types of U.S. military hardware. Click on "U.S. Land Warfare Systems" for details on specific tanks and other military vehicles.

http://www.military.cz
Online Czech archive of military technology, including information and pictures about the most famous tanks and AFVs used in World War II.

http://www.onwar.com/tanks
This site contains historical and technical information about AFVs in use during, and immediately prior to, World War II.

http://www.tankmuseum.org/home.html
Here you can find information about tanks of the world—and more about The Tank Museum in Bovington, Great Britain.

⚠

INTERNET SAFETY

Always follow these guidelines for a fun and safe journey through cyberspace:

1. Ask your parents for permission before you go online.

2. Spend time with your parents online and show them your favorite sites.

3. Mail your family's E-mail address, even if you have your own (only give your personal address to someone you trust).

4. Do not reply to E-mails if you feel they are strange or upsetting.

5. Do not use your real last name when you are online.

6. Never plan to meet "cyber friends" in person without your parents' permission.

7. Never give anyone your password.

8. Never give anyone your home address or telephone number.

9. Do not send scanned pictures of yourself unless your parents approve.

10. Leave a website right away if you find something that is offensive or upsetting. Talk to your parents about it.

Copyright © 2003 Chrysalis Books Group

Editorial Director: Honor Head
Art Director: Sophie Wilkins
Senior Editor: Rasha Elsaeed
Project Editor: Leon Gray
Designer: Scott Gibson
Picture Researcher: Terry Forshaw

ISBN 1-93233-355-X
Library of Congress Control Number 2003102605

Printed in China

Distributed in the United States by Smart Apple Media, 1980 Lookout Drive, North Mankato, MN 56003

CONTENTS

THE TANK CLOSE-UP

Tanks have played a role in all the major ground battles since 1916. The first British tanks were little, armor-plated tractors with basic field-gun or machine-gun armaments. Since World War II (1939–1945), there have been many improvements to tank designs, and their huge size and elaborate designs became surplus to requirements. On the following pages you can find out about all kinds of tracked vehicles, from the earliest armored personnel carriers (APCs) right through to the very latest combat tanks.

MEGA MBT
No single weapons system on the battlefield has to face such an array of threats as the main battle tank (MBT). These vehicles face attack by aircraft, other tanks, and armored fighting vehicles (AFVs), mines, and ground-launched, antitank guided weapons.

Observation periscope

The main armament of this Leopard 2 MBT is a 120mm smoothbore gun.

The main gun of the Leopard 2 can fire a range of ammunition, including the new armor-piercing, fin-stabilized, discarding sabot (APFSDS) rounds.

Track

Ernest Swinton

As a British war correspondent on the Western Front during World War II, Sir Ernest Dunlop Swinton had witnessed the deaths of thousands of Allied infantry soldiers at the hands of German machine gunners. Swinton first suggested the development of what became known as the "tank" when he saw a tractor towing a gun. The British military developed a prototype, and then Prime Minister Lloyd George immediately authorized full-scale production. These early tanks left the assembly line too late for use in the Somme offensive, but their battlefield debut came in Flers in September 1916. They have been used ever since.

The turret is reinforced at the front with spaced armor for added protection.

LIGHTEN UP!

At the beginning of World War II, a typical tank, such as the British Cruiser Mk 1V, weighed around 16.5 tons. By the end of the war, tanks such as the German Tiger 11 weighed a massive 78.2 tons! During the 1950s and 1960s, manufacturers lowered the weight of their vehicles to 44 tons to increase their mobility.

Hull

Like the turret, the hull and side skirts of the Leopard 2 have spaced armor for increased protection.

Side skirt

MEGA FACT
The first great tank battle took place in Cambrai, northern France, on November 20, 1917.

MAIN BATTLE TANKS

Until 1916, many of the great battles were fought and won by ships at sea. Ground combat was hard work for soldiers with limited weapons and mobility. The tank changed life on the battlefield dramatically. With the tank's combination of firepower, maneuverability, and protection, soldiers could travel into previously inaccessible areas. One tank could cause more damage than a whole company of foot soldiers. But tank manufacturers had to strike a balance between armor, firepower, and mobility to be truly effective fighting machines.

MEGA BATTLE
During the Battle of Kursk, from July to September in 1943, 2,700 German tanks fought against 3,300 Soviet tanks.

⊕ **WHAT'S IN A NAME?**
How did the tank get its name? One theory suggests that when the first tanks were shipped from Britain to France, hidden under canvas sheets, inquisitive soldiers were told that they were transporting large water tanks.

Little Willie

The first prototype tank, or "land ship," as it was then known, was demonstrated to British military experts on September 11, 1915. The prototype, called "Little Willie," weighed around 15.5 tons and was powered by a Daimler engine. On even terrain, the 12-foot-long track frames carried a three-man crew at an average speed of just over 3 miles per hour. But the average speed dropped to less than 2 miles per hour over uneven terrain, and Little Willie could not cross broad trenches.

ARMOR AND ATTACK

Major improvements in tank armor appeared in the 1980s. Some armor systems make antitank missiles explode outward on impact. New armament includes guns that fire guided missiles and shells made of hard materials that punch straight through enemy tanks.

I CAN DO THAT!

Modern armored fighting vehicles (AFVs) have mostly replaced the big, heavy tanks of the past. Smaller and lighter than their predecessors, many AFVs can perform multiple roles during combat and peacetime ground operations.

MEGA BATTLE
During the Middle East War in 1967, 1,000 Israeli tanks battled against 2,050 Egyptian, Jordanian, and Syrian tanks.

CHIEFTAIN MBT

The Chieftain Main Battle Tank (MBT) has been one of the most successful postwar tanks, with its heavy steel armor and large 120mm main gun. The Chieftain MBT was phased out of the British Army in 1996 after 30 years of service. A number of specialized variants are still in service, including the Armored Recovery Vehicle (ARV), Armored Vehicle-Launched Bridge (AVLB), and Armored Vehicle Royal Engineer (AVRE).

M1 ABRAMS MBT

The first Abrams M1 MBT was in operation by 1982. Three years later, there were 2,380 M1s. During Operation Desert Storm, the United States military deployed nearly 2,000 M1s to the Persian Gulf, where they destroyed most of the Iraqi's Soviet tank fleet. The 105mm main gun on the M1, and the 120mm gun on the M1A1 and M1A2, combined with the powerful turbine engine and almost impenetrable armor, means that the M1 Abrams can attack or defend against large concentrations of heavily armored forces.

MERKAVA MK3 BAZ

After years of hands-on combat experience in the Arab–Israeli conflict, Major-General Israel Tal designed the Merkava MBT. Most modern MBTs have the engine at the rear, but the Merkava has the engine at the front of the tank. This provides a special protective umbrella for the crew. The Merkava Mk 1 entered service against Syrian forces in 1982. The Merkava Mk 3 entered service in 1990. New features include a higher-power main gun, a laser-warning system, and new armor, suspension, and transmission systems.

LECLERC MBT

The Leclerc MBT came into service with the French Army in 1992 and the United Arab Emirates in 1995. This tank includes a gun with an automatic loading system, which makes it possible to fire when the tank is moving and at a rate of up to six shots per minute. The Leclerc can engage enemy vehicles on any terrain, day or night, whatever the weather. The multipurpose armored protection, stealth features, agility, and long-range capability make the Leclerc a truly awesome fighter.

T-90 MBT

The T-90 entered production in 1994 and is the latest in the T-series of Russian tanks. The main armament is the 125mm 2A46M smoothbore gun, which can fire a range of ammunition, including laser-guided 9M119M "Refleks" antitank missiles and AT-11 Sniper antitank guided missiles (ATGM). The T-90 has a four-stroke diesel engine with a multifuel capability. Like all Russian MBTs, the T-90 creates its own smoke screen by spraying diesel fuel into the main exhaust outlet.

MEGA FACT
The Soviet Army was the first military power to develop a three-crew tank with an autoloader, replacing the loader to save weight and height.

ARIETE MBT

The Italian Army employs the 119,050-pound Ariete tank to engage stationary and moving targets. The main gun is a 44-caliber, 120mm smoothbore gun, which fires armor-piercing, fin-stabilized, discarding sabot (APFSDS) and high explosive, antitank (HEAT) rounds. A nuclear, biological, and chemical (NBC) protection system guards against NBC attack. The tank is powered by a turbocharged Fiat V-12 MTCA, 12-cylinder diesel engine.

Sherman Tank World War II

The United States M4 Sherman medium tank was the major AFV of the Allied forces during World War II, serving on every major front. By the end of the war, factory workers in 11 assembly plants in the United States were turning out almost 2,000 tanks a month. Each M4 weighed about 67,240 pounds and carried a crew of five soldiers. The main armament was a 75mm M3 gun, with a 2in M3 smoke mortar in the turret roof and several machine guns fixed in various positions on the body of the vehicle.

LEOPARD 2 MBT

The Leopard series of German tanks were developed in the 1960s. The Leopard 1 was first produced in 1963 and its upgrade, Leopard 2, followed in 1979. Leopard 2 includes a new 120mm L55 smoothbore gun to replace the shorter 120mm L44 smoothbore gun on the Leopard 1. The new armament supports the new APFSDS-T ammunition. The Leopard 2 also includes the Integrated Command and Information System (ICIS) and can be sealed for NBC warfare. More than 8,000 Leopard 1 and 2 MBTs have been fielded by 18 countries, including 11 NATO nations and Australia, Austria, Brazil, and Chile.

MEGA FACT
Late-model Soviet tanks have an interior lining of a synthetic material containing lead, which provides some protection against nuclear fallout, neutron radiation, and electromagnetic pulse (EMP).

LIGHT TANKS

Armies around the world have invested a lot of time and money developing tracked vehicles that are smaller, lighter, easier to crew, cheaper to maintain, and more affordable than the heavily armed and armored MBTs. Light tanks are often deployed in situations where MBTs are impractical or unavailable, for instance, against unsophisticated enemy vehicles and in policing operations. Light tanks first came into service in the 1950s and 1960s. Many are still used today, although they are often described as destroyers or reconnaissance vehicles.

MEGA FACT
In 1952, Soviet PT76 amphibious vehicles were the first tanks to use hydrojets as a means of water propulsion.

MEGA FACT
The Soviet Union and communist Eastern European formed the Warsaw Pact in response to the admission of West Germany into NATO.

Alvis Striker SP ATGW

As soon as tanks appeared in World War I, armies began working on ways to stop or destroy these machines using antitank weapons. Antitank guided weapons (ATGWs) may be single-shot, one-man weapons, or they may have a crew, such as the British Alvis Striker SP ATGW. The Alvis Striker fires a wire-guided, Swingfire antitank missile. Most modern ATGWs are wire-guided. This reliable guidance system cannot be jammed by the enemy.

MULTIWHEELED MOBILITY

For many years, most wheeled AFVs outside the former Warsaw Pact countries were of the 4x4 type. However, there has been a trend toward developing 6x6 and 8x8 AFVs with increased payloads and greater cross-country mobility.

MEGA FACT
In 1904, the first armored car—the Charron Girardot et Voigt—was built in France.

LIGHT AFVs

Many countries already use light AFVs fleets. Wheeled vehicles such as the Light Armored Vehicle LAV-25 (shown left) have lower operating costs than most MBTs, and they have greater strategic mobility and are also easier to transport by air.

LAV-25

The U.S. Army and Marine Corps was assigned the first LAV-25s in 1983. These are all-terrain, all-weather 8x8 vehicles have a maximum speed of 62 miles per hour on the ground. As an amphibious vehicle, the LAV-25 is powered by two propellers mounted at the rear of the hull, which can reach a top speed of 6.5 miles per hour through the water.

M24 CHAFFEE LIGHT

The M24 Chaffee is considered to be one of the best light tanks of World War II. The first of these vehicles was produced in 1943, and the U.S. Army placed a large order soon after trials proved the effectiveness of these new tanks. By the end of the war, the manufacturers Cadillac and Massey Harris had produced a total of 4,070 M24s. The first to reach Europe in late 1944 were used as reconnaissance vehicles. The M24 Chaffee remained in service in the U.S. Army until 1953 when it was replaced by the M41 Bulldog.

AMX-13 LIGHT TANK/RECCE VEHICLE

Work on the French AMX-13 began a year after the end of World War II, and it has proved to be one of the most successful postwar tank designs in the world. Originally, it was designed to be transportable by aircraft and provide airborne forces with medium-fire support. The AMX-13 soon became the standard light tank of the French Army, where it was employed as a tank destroyer and reconnaissance vehicle. All AMX-13 have a similar layout: the driver sits front left, with the engine to his right and the turret at the rear.

MEGA FIRST
The first commercial tracked vehicle was a converted steam agricultural tractor, built by the American Holt Manufacturing Company in 1906.

T-26

The T-26 light tank was the Soviet version of the Vickers-Armstrong 6.5-ton Tank. Initially, the T-26 was both a single-turret and twin-turret tank, but production centered on the single-turret version after 1933. By the time production ceased in 1939, more than 6,500 T-26 variants had rolled off the assembly lines.

Armies need their tanks to have amphibious capabilities so that they can continue advancing without the need for cumbersome and slow-moving bridging equipment to help them cross waterways. Some light vehicles can float, and most MBTs rely on flotation mechanisms to help them cross the water. However, most tanks are capable of submerged fording, which means that they can cross rivers approximately a foot deep.

DUKW

The DUKW was a large, six-wheel-drive, amphibious landing craft that was first used by the U.S. Army and Marine Corps in World War II. This vehicle proved to be so reliable that the United States manufactured more than 20,000 DUKWs during the conflict. The DUKW was used to transport equipment from supply ships in transportation areas offshore, to supply depots and fighting units on the beach. It could maintain a speed of 50 miles per hour on land and 5 knots at sea.

Cadillac Gage Stingray LT

Textron Marine & Land Systems (formerly Cadillac Gage) developed the Stingray as an extremely mobile light tank with the firepower of an MBT. The Stingray fires a range of ammunition, including British and U.S. APFSDS rounds and NATO 105mm ordnance. In terms of mobility, the Stingray can climb gradients of up to 60 percent and cross vertical obstacles up to 32 inches high, and water depths to 42 inches. These features make this tank an attractive addition to the armies of countries throughout the world.

BRDM-2

The BRDM-2 is a fully armored, four-wheel drive, amphibious reconnaissance vehicle with a 140-horsepower, V-8 engine, and full NBC protection capability. The basic BRDM-2 reconnaissance vehicle is distinguished by its turret. The conical turret, which mounts two machine guns, has no top-hatch opening. This model carries a crew of four soldiers: the commander, gunner, driver, and codriver. The BRDM-2 was first deployed in 1966, and it has generally replaced the earlier BRDM in the former Soviet Union and other Warsaw Pact nations.

ARMORED PERSONNEL CARRIERS

Many modern tracked vehicles used by today's armies serve different purposes and can be classified under more than one type. For instance, the German Marder and the British Warrior are classed as both APCs and Armored Infantry Fighting Vehicles (AIFVs). Wheeled APCs are widely used in United Nations peace-keeping operations, because they protect against rifle and machine-gun fire as well as shell fragments.

MEGA FACT
The idea of an AFV appeared in rough drawings by the Italian artist Leonardo da Vinci in 1482. Leonardo's AFV was propelled by a crew that operated geared hand cranks and fired muskets through slits.

Hidden Armor

All tanks and AFVs are camouflaged to blend in with their surroundings, which makes them more difficult to see from a distance, especially by passing enemy aircraft. Extra armor is also added to many tanks to protect them against enemy fire, but this increased weight inevitably slows them down. The M981 (shown right) is an M113 series tank with extra armor added to the top. To avoid adding to much weight to the vehicle, the armor is made of aluminum.

TANK TRANSPORTERS

The British Ministry of Defence has placed an order with the consortium FASTTRAX to manufacture a new fleet of huge tank transporters. The transporters—known as Heavy Equipment Transporters (HETs)—are based on the U.S. tank-transporter system with a similar name, and will be collectively capable of carrying more than 90 tanks into combat zones at speeds of up to 80 miles per hour. The FASTTRAX consortium will own, operate and maintain the fleet of 92 transporters. The service is planned to commence in 2003.

MEGA FACT
The U.S. Army has purchased 1,179 Heavy Equipment Transporter System (HETS) trucks and trailers since the contract was completed in 1992.

A DUCK TO WATER

A number of specialized versions of the M113 series are in service with the Norwegian Army, including the NM142. This tank has a one-man Armored Launching Turret with two Tube-Launched, Optically-Tracked, Wire Guided (TOW) ATGW in the ready-to-launch position. This amphibious vehicle is propelled through the water by the movement of its tracks.

M113

The first M113 tanks were operational by 1962. With more than 80,000 vehicles built in the United States, and M113 production also under license in Italy, this tank is now the most widely used military vehicle in the world—in service in 50 countries. The M113 was the first AFV to be built using aircraft-quality aluminum. The General Motors Detroit Diesel 6V-53 engine has an output of 275 horsepower at 2,800 revolutions per minute.

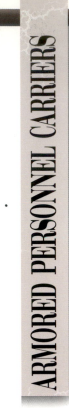

MEGA FACT
The British War Office saw the first true AFV in 1902, when the Simms "War Car" was demonstrated to the military.

WARRIOR APC/AIFV

The armament of the Warrior can be adapted for a range of combat conditions, but a 30mm Rarden cannon and a 7.62 Boeing M242 chain gun are typical specifications. There are a number of variants of the Warrior, including a mechanized recovery vehicle and mortar carrier. As an AIFV, the Warrior is operated by a commander, driver, and gunner, with room for seven soldiers.

MEGA FACT
The M113 was the first "battle taxi" developed to transport infantry forces on the battlefield.

MARDER APC/AIFV

The first Marders were delivered to the German Army in 1970. Since then, over 3,000 vehicles have rolled off the assembly lines. The all-welded, steel hull of this tank provides the driver and troop—a total of eight personnel—with complete protection from small-arms fire and shell splinters. The two-man turret is in the middle of the vehicle, and the troop compartment is in the rear, with two rows of infantry soldiers on each side. The armament consists of a 20mm Rheinmetall Mk 20 Rh 202 cannon and a 7.62mm machine gun. This tank is also has smoke grenade launchers to the left of the cannon.

BTR-60 APC

The Soviet Army unveiled the eight-wheeled BTR-60 just four years after the first in the line of Soviet APCs—the BTR-50P—came into service in 1957. The BTR-60 was the standard APC of the Soviet Naval Infantry (the Soviet Marine Corps). Throughout the 1960s, the BTR-60 was improved until the 8x8 BTR-70 finally replaced it.

RECONNAISSANCE

Reconnaissance vehicles provide the military with important intelligence information. They are sent out ahead of troops and AFVs to survey the local area, secretly observe the enemy, and report their findings back to base. Modern reconnaissance vehicles can protect and defend themselves when necessary. They are heavily armored and carry a variety of weapons systems, including machine guns and mortar weapons.

A CLASS OF THEIR OWN?

The classification of tanks into specific groups, for example, AIFVs, APCs, light tanks, and MBTs, can be confusing. What is classed as a reconnaissance vehicle by military officials in one country may be classed as a light tank by officials in another country.

German Panzer Units of WWII

German forces used the first of the Panzer series of tanks, Panzer I, during the invasion of Poland in 1939. During the conquests of 1940–1942, the faster, more powerful Panzer II saw active service. In 1943, the German Army took control of the Italian M15/42 medium tank, designating them PzKpfw III tanks. These formed the bulk of the Panzer Divisionen during the early war years. The Panzer IV—the workhorse Panzer tank—was extremely successful on the battlefield, but a final model, the Panzer V, was developed to counter the threat of the Soviet T-34 model.

MEGA FACT
The Scorpion is also deployed as a light tank in the armies of many countries, including Belgium, Indonesia, Iran, Ireland, Nigeria, Oman, the Phillipines, Spain, Thailand, and the United Arab Emirates.

⊕ SUPER SCORPION!

The Scorpion reconnaissance vehicle (shown left), officially the first of the British military's Combat Vehicle Reconnaissance (Tracked) (CVR(T)) series, was developed by Alvis in the Great Britain. The first units appeared in 1972. In 1979, the British RAF Regiment acquired 150 Scorpions in different versions for the protection of air bases in Germany. By 1999, over 3,500 Scorpions had been built for British military use and the export market.

SCORPION

In May 1970, the Scorpion was officially retained for the British Army's reconnaissance units and were designated Combat Vehicle Reconnaissance (Tracked) (CVR(T)). Scorpion vehicles come with a variety of optional equipment, including NBC protection, thermal night-vision equipment, a powered turret, air-conditioning, and flotation screens. Scorpion vehicles were at the forefront of the 7th Armoured Brigade of the Desert Rats during the 1991 Gulf War. They continue to serve the United Nations peacekeeping forces in Bosnia.

SHADOW RST-V

This 4x4 hybrid, electric-drive vehicle with reconnaissance, surveillance, targeting, and C3I (command, control, communications, and intelligence) capability is coupled with integrated stealth features. The Shadow RST-V can be equipped in a range of mission variants, including air defense, antiarmor, battlefield ambulance, forward observer, light strike, logistics, mortar weapons carrier, personnel carrier, and reconnaissance. Bulletproof windows can also be installed.

MEGA FACT
The Luchs has the same power and speed capability whether it travels backward or forward.

BA-64

The BA-64 was the first Soviet armored car with four-wheel drive. The driver's observation visor was made of removable, bulletproof glass, and the 7.62mm Degtyarev's machine gun was mounted on a universal machine-gun ring to allow 360 degree rotation. BA-64s and BA-64Bs were used in all major operations and battles of the Eastern Front. A total of 8,174 armored cars from both types were accepted for the Red Army. The last 62 vehicles were manufactured in 1946.

MEGA FACT
The Scimitar variant of the Scorpion CVR(T) is used by the British Army as an APC to carry specialist troops, such as mortar fire control and antiaircraft personnel.

LUCHS

The German-manufactured Luchs A2 is an 8x8, armored amphibious reconnaissance vehicle capable of carrying five crew members and a variety of weapons systems. The engine is in a separate compartment at the back, and this is partitioned from the crew's quarters by gas-tight, welded bulkheads and fitted with an automatic fire-suppression system.

The British Royal Navy and the Belgian military were the first to use armored cars with machine guns in 1914. The interwar period saw the development of six- and eight-wheeled armored cars and half-track vehicles, which had tracks to the rear and wheels at the front. Today, AFVs are used for many military tasks, including air-defense protection, recovery, and support vehicles, combat headquarters, NBC detection vehicles, and APCs.

MEGA FACT

The most famous antitank gun of World War II was the 88mm/Flak 41, simply known as "the 88." This heavy-duty German weapon was designed and built as an antiaircraft gun.

MEGA FACT

The first major tank victory since World War II was won by Israel against Egypt during the Suez Crisis in 1956.

M110—Howitzer

The 203mm M110-series, self-propelled, heavy artillery cannon was the heaviest field artillery unit in the U.S. Army and Marine Corps. This mobile howitzer could fire enhanced radiation "neutron" nuclear warheads, but they did not provide ballistic protection for the 12-man crew. A total of around 2,000 M110-series howitzers were built. The M110A1/A2s, which were active in the Vietnam conflict, superceded the earlier model in the early 1960s. The system was phased out by the U.S. military in the 1990s, but it is still in service with the armies of other nations.

SCOUTING AROUND!

The Bradley Fighting Vehicle System includes the M2 Infantry Fighting Vehicle, the M3 Cavalry Fighting Vehicle, and the M6 Bradley Linebacker. Since 1981, around 6,720 vehicles of all types have been deployed by the U.S. and Saudi Arabian armies. The M3 performs scout missions and carries three crew, in addition to two scouts. The U.S. Army Bradley upgrade program includes improvements based on operational experience in the 1991 Gulf War. The first upgrades—the M2A3/M3A3—entered service in April 2000.

BRADLEY M3

The U.S. military authorized full-scale production of the M2A3/M3A3 Bradley in May 2001 following two years of low-rate production in response to the Bradley upgrade program. The main armament of the M2A3/M3A3 Bradley is a Boeing 25mm M242 Bushmaster chain gun. This AFV comes with two M257 smoke grenade dischargers, each loaded with four smoke grenades. The vehicle is equipped with a VTA-903T engine, and the hydromechanical transmission HMPT-500 provides three speed ranges. The engines give a maximum speed of 41 miles per hour. All Bradleys are amphibious.

MEGA FACT
Welded aluminum and spaced laminate armor protects the hull of the M3 Bradley.

BMP-3

The Soviet BMP-3 is the last in the BMP series of infantry combat vehicles produced in the late 1980s. The tracked, amphibious BMP-3 is designed to engage armored ground and air targets when it is stationary, on the move, and afloat. The main armament is a 100mm 2A70 semiautomatic rifled gun/missile launcher. The vehicle is powered a V-shaped UTD-29 diesel engine, which produces up to 500 horsepower. It is still in service with the Russian Army, although it has faced some criticism from military experts.

PIRANHA

The Piranha series of light armored vehicles was designed by Mowag of Switzerland in the late 1960s. These amphibious vehicles come in a number of different wheel combinations, including 4x4, 6x6, 8x8, and 10x10 configurations. They can protect its occupants against small-arms fire and shell splinters.

The Piranha Armored Combat Vehicle (ACV) is part of the Swedish Navy's coastal artillery brigade.

WARRIOR

Although the APCs designed in the 1960s were capable of performing specialized roles, they did not have the armor or firepower needed to fight on the modern battlefield. In 1986, the Mechanized Combat Vehicle 80 (MCV-80) went into production. Given the name "Warrior," this APC could protect against indirect artillery fragments, direct machine-gun fire, and also offered firepower for general combat support. The Warrior became operational in 1988, and was used by the British Army in the 1991 Gulf War.

29

GLOSSARY

AAV
Advanced Amphibious Assault Vehicle.

AFV
Armored Fighting Vehicle, tanks, APCs, and any vehicle protected by armor plate.

AIFV
Armored Infantry Fighting Vehicle.

AMPHIBIOUS
Vehicle capable of traveling on land and sea.

APC
Armored Personnel Carrier. An AFV designed to carry an infantry squad.

ARV
Armored Recovery Vehicle.

ATGW
Antitank Guided Weapon.

CV
Combat Vehicle.

CVRT
Combat Vehicle Reconnaissance Tracked.

FV
Fighting Vehicle.

HEAT
High-Explosive Antitank.

IFV
Infantry Fighting Vehicle.

LAV
Light Assault Vehicle.

MBT
Main Battle Tank.

MRAV
Multi-Role Armored Vehicle.

NBC
Nuclear, Biological, and Chemical.

PANZER
The abbreviation of the WW2 *Panzerkampfwagen*—armored war vehicle. The German word for tank.

RECONNAISSANCE
The act of finding out any information that will help in battle.

SP GUN
Self-propelled gun, artillery mounted on an AFV chassis, which protects the crew and ensures mobility.

SSM
Surface-to-surface missile, any missile launched from the ground against another target that is also on the ground.

TOW
Tube-Launched, Optically-Tracked, Wire Guided.

INDEX

Military Magazines:

✗ Air Classics Magazine   ✗ Bulletin of Atomic Scientists   ✗ Military Trader
✗ Air & Space Magazine   ✗ Civil War Times   ✗ Military Heritage
✗ America's Civil War   ✗ Military History   ✗ Navy Times
✗ Army Times   ✗ MHQ   ✗ World War II

Picture Credits

Front and back cover top (far left), TRH; (centre), MARS; (centre right), TRH; 5, Hulton Archive; 9 (both), TRH; 10 (top), Novosti; 11(bottom), TRH; 15 (top), MARS; 22-24 (all), TRH; 29 (top), TRH; back cover main image, TRH.
All other pictures Chrysalis Images